AZERBAIJANI JEWS IN SPORTS

SECOND EDITION

ASIF BAYRAMOV

Fulton Books
Meadville, PA

Published by Fulton Books 2024

ISBN 979-8-88982-590-6 (paperback)
ISBN 979-8-88982-592-0 (digital)

Printed in the United States of America

Reviewer:
Professor Mikhail Y. Agarunov

Asif Bayramov
Azerbaijani Jews In Sports

The book describes the migration routes of Jews in Azerbaijan and their places of residence. Contributing to the science, arts, and culture of the Jews, they do not neglect the development of sports in Azerbaijan. It's a fact that they were once pioneers in some kinds of modern sports. Their contribution to the development of Azerbaijani sports is irreplaceable. This little book is designed to show who's who in the history of sports in our sovereign state. The participation of the Mountain Jews in the development of Azerbaijani sports is of great importance. This sports book is recommended for schoolchildren, students, teachers, and professors.

Jerusalem, March 20, 2023

Mr. Asif Bayramov

Dear Asif,

I was grateful to receive your book, Azerbaijan Jews in Sport, along with your warm note, and relay my fond appreciation for the thoughtful gesture of sharing it with my office. It is clear that Israel and the Jewish nation hold a meaningful place in your heart, and I am pleased to learn that it is a connection that has inspired you, particularly toward reaching the next generation .

As you know, the State of Israel deeply values its relationship with the Republic of Azerbaijan. While we share common interests and values at the geostrategic and political level, it is people like you who help support our bilateral ties by being ambassadors of goodwill and friendship .

I thank you again for your kind gesture and wish you the very best.

Yours Sincerely,

Isaac Herzog
President of the State of Israel

CONTENTS

-

 Review of Professor Moses Baker, Fellow of Institute for Human Rights, Azerbaijani Academy of Science

This work is the first attempt to create a holistic picture of the participation of representatives of the Jewish community of Azerbaijan in various sports. Until now, this topic has not been touched upon in any way. We are all used to seeing Jews in science, culture, and art as engineers and technicians, doctors, writers, and composers. And in this regard, Azerbaijan is no exception. On the contrary, as a percentage of the population, Jews found themselves in an even better situation than other union republics of the former USSR. But Jews in sports… Few people were interested in this question since it was completely unusual to see a Jewish football player, wrestler, boxer, honored coach of the USSR, or master of sports. Chess, yes! And here in Azerbaijan, there were quite a number of international masters, grandmasters, and champions of the USSR and even of the world.

That is why the fact that A. Bayramov's book was published is of lasting value for us, both as a part of the history of the Jewish community in Azerbaijan and as a factor in the special conditions that have developed in the republic, where an atmosphere of tolerance and multiculturalism has always reigned. This is probably why no one is surprised that the author of the study is Asif Bayramov, an Azerbaijani by nationality and a Muslim by religion. The book brought to your attention covers a significant period in the history of sports in the Republic of Azerbaijan and is a clear example of the fact that sport is a symbol of peace, friendship, and unity among people.

INTRODUCTION

-

The reader may ask what made me, a refugee from Armenia, write such a book about the Jews. The point is that our fate has been similar. In 1988, as a result of Armenian aggression, hundreds of thousands of people were expelled from their homes (1905–1907; 1914–1915; 1917–1918; 1937–1939; 1947–1949), and one of the two hundred thousand refugee families was my family.

I had heard different opinions about the Jews, both pleasant and not so pleasant. So I decided to think about this matter. Every nation has its own drawbacks. As for the Jews, as far as I understand, the only shortcoming they are suffering from is their honesty, truthfulness, and punctuality. I think they have been suffering from this characteristic feature.

The first time I got acquainted with the Jews was when I was first introduced to them in St. Petersburg, Russian Federation after service in the Soviet Army. They made a very positive impression on me. A closer acquaintance with these wonderful people helped me better understand our own problems.

In 1992, I moved to Baku to live there permanently. I made many friends among the Jews. In 1993, for the first time in Baku, I was one of the organizers of the exhibition "History, Culture, and Daily Life of the Jews Living in Azerbaijan and Dagestan." In organizing the exhibition, I met the Jewish athletes.

In this regard, there was a desire to do further research. The idea of writing a book about the Jews of Azerbaijan in sports occurred to me during my ongoing work. I began to study the archives and found out that many interesting materials had been lost. Very little information about the role of Jews in sports has been preserved in the archive.

I had to look for old Azerbaijani Jews to collect the necessary research information from their stories. It was very difficult, as many of them had already died.

I cannot judge how interesting the book will be. I did my best.

I would be happy to hear any criticism and appreciation from readers.

The author is ready to express his opinion, facts, and everything else on the topic as a part of his intellect.

I am not seeking ways to convince somebody or change people's opinions. The main purpose of this book is to interest, inform, and invite people to think. It is known that distrusting the reader is a catastrophe for the author[1]. If you don't trust the addressee, you'd better not write to him.

Now let's start.

Coming to the end of our sports history, the reader will know more than now.

---

[1] Author is a Latin word that means "multiplying" or "growing." That's how people name those who multiply in the broad sense of the word and are the wealth of people.

MIGRATION PATHS OF JEWS IN AZERBAIJAN

Historically, Azerbaijan has always been a unique state in which different people and religions coexisted for centuries. Fire worshipers, Christians, Muslims, Jews, Molokans, Baptists, and many others have inhabited this ancient land.

Jews came here a long time ago. No one can say the exact date of their settlement in Azerbaijan. Some time ago, Professor R. Goyushev reported that during the excavation of the ancient Shabran lands, he discovered the ruins of a synagogue there. Of course, before the destruction of the First Temple in 586 BC, Jews could barely exist in Azerbaijan. Even as captives of the Babylonian kingdom, the Jews probably were not familiar with this mysterious territory. After the liberation of the Jews from slavery in 538 BC, most of them returned to their homeland—Judea. Only a small part remained in the new Persian empire, where Jews achieved a high position.

According to the "Megillah" Jews, who lived in 120 areas of the vast Persian empire, the structure of this state included the southern part of Azerbaijan. The first Jewish settlers may have settled there at that time. In any case, Jewish merchants had certainly been to these areas. Persian rulers frequently used the tactic of settling conquered countries with new settlers, among which could have been Jewish colonies. Thus, we can imagine how Persian-speaking Jews settled in Azerbaijan. They are known as Mountain Jews. Many of them settled in Derbent and the mountains of Dagestan. The Juhut-Gala region between Guba and Derbent, centered on Aba-Sava, was the place where Jewish theology and Jewish literature in Hebrew flourished. The city of Guba is located in the north of Azerbaijan. Derbent is a former Azerbaijani city located on the territory of the Russian Federation.

Auls (small villages) of the Mountain Jews were situated at the border of eternal snow (hence, the name "Mountain Jews"). The Guba, Kusary, Devechi, and other regions of Azerbaijan are rich with old cemeteries with monuments of six-pointed stars and Hebrew inscriptions. In the Middle Ages, Jews were engaged in trade and commerce. Some of them passed through the Derbent passage, penetrated into the Northern Caspian Sea, and settled in Arkel, Makhachkala, Hasavyurte, and the capital of the Khazar Khanate—Itil.

In the eighth century, the head of the Khazar Khaganate adopted Judaism as its official religion. However, the new religion was taken very seriously. In our opinion, Judaism of the Karaime trend was initially adopted by people, and only during the reign of Joseph was there an attempt to "correct the belief." However, this state did not last long, and the capital itself of the Khaganate soon immersed itself under the waters of the Caspian Sea.

Actually, it should be noted that the Turkish people were traditionally very kind toward the Jewish settlers, whom they saw as very necessary and useful people. Just remember that it was in the Ottoman Empire in 1492 when most refugees were from Spain and then Portugal.

After the catastrophe of Spanish Jewry, the Jews of the Iberian Peninsula were rescued by the

Turkish Empire, where Azerbaijan also took an active part. Having escaped from the Spanish Inquisition, Sephardic Jews gave Sephardic Nusach to the Jews of Eastern Transcaucasia, where they had great influence over the flourishing Jewish culture in Azerbaijan in the seventeenth and eighteenth centuries.

In the eighteenth century, Fatali Khan in Guba invited the Jews living in Dagestan and neighboring khanates to live in his territories. From mountain villages and small villages, the Jews moved to the area of Guba, where they formed a compact settlement now known as the "Red Sloboda." People built synagogues and many houses and settled down in the hospitable Guba Khanate. Local authorities treated the Jews very loyally, appreciating their hard work, honesty, and knowledge. Many of them engaged in trade and commerce. The labor of tinsmiths, shoemakers, weavers, and goldsmiths brought Khanate wealth and prosperity.

In the middle of the nineteenth century, with the development of the oil industry in Baku, the Jews began to move from Georgia and the western regions of the enormous Russian Empire. Ashkenazi Jews were the first to appear in the so-called "Pale" in 1832. They were mostly merchants and craftsmen and settled, as usual, near and around the synagogue or house of worship. There were the first Jewish neighborhoods. The followers of the two branches of Judaism began to live in Azerbaijani lands—the Ashkenazi and Sefardi. The Ashkenazi community prevailed in Baku. There was a constant influx of people from the western regions of the empire. The positive attitude of the local population and the lack of discrimination contributed to the growth of the Jewish population. Moreover, they now had the ability to realize their potential and obtain jobs as a result of the oil boom. At the end of the nineteenth century, there appeared quite a significant stratum of Jewish engineers, technically integrating into Azerbaijan with the people who worked in the oil fields—the Rothschild brothers and Nobel brothers. Doctors, engineers, lawyers and Industrialists - these are the main sphere where the Jews found their application. At that time, the Jew population of Baku was 9689 people, or 4.5% of the total population.

In the days of the Azerbaijan Democratic Republic, Jews were represented in the Parliament, and the Minister of Health of the first government was the famous children's doctor, Professor E. A. Gindes.

In 1920, after the Sovietization of Azerbaijan, many in the wealthier sectors were forced to emigrate. All noncommunist parties and organizations were banned. Thus began a struggle against Zionism; religious instruction and education were banned. Generations of people were uprooted from their culture and traditions. Indoor synagogues built in 1910 housed a Jewish theater and various educational institutions. All of this, of course, did not contribute to the preservation of the Jewish culture, which gradually began to erode under the influence of the "new community"—the Soviet people.

Still, life was going on. Many Jews enthusiastically joined in building a new life. Jews became the commissars, managers and directors of large companies, musicians, doctors, and scientists. Old Baku people remember well the musicians: Bella Davidovich, L. Weinstein, M. Brenner, S. E. Shefferlinga, and S. Krongolda; doctors: T. Listengarten, C. Guzman, Zhitnitsky, and Khaldeeva; lawyers: F. Enkena, V. Gadasevicha, A. Goldman, and many others. A simple listing of names alone would take up too much space. During World War II, the Jews contributed to the victory over fascism. Heroes of the Soviet Union Shakhnovich M., S. Levine, and others lived in Baku.

After the collapse of the USSR and the events of 1990, many Jews emigrated to Israel, the US, and Germany. In the pre-perestroika period in Azerbaijan, there were about 80,000 Jews—of these Ashkenazi (50,000) and Mountain Jews (about 2 to 2.5 thousand). Now the picture has changed. There are only about 6,000 Ashkenazi Jews left, about 16,000 Mountain Jews, and several hundred Georgians. All figures are approximate. Today, thanks to the balanced national policy of the Azerbaijani leadership, many Jews have returned to their homeland.

We mentioned above that Azerbaijan has been the homeland of two branches of the Jewish people. People whose ancestors lived together for twenty centuries under different conditions and partially accepted cultures are close to each other not only by their origin but also by their common spiritual basis—religion. Judaism as a belief system and as a rule of life originated in Mesopotamia in Ur, where the patriarch Abraham, the leader of one of the Semitic Aramaic tribes, was a forerunner of the idea of one God. This idea was crystallized over hundreds of years. Only after the exodus of the Jews from Egypt and the Prophet Moses receiving the Torah at Mount Sinai did Judaism become a written code of laws. In addition, an important part of Jewish law was the Halacha, which gives an explanation of each case of family laws and traditions, strictly prescribing total adherence for every Jew.

HISTORICAL OVERVIEW

Sports such as javelin throwing, archery, weight lifting, and similar gymnastic exercises were the main sports for boys.

In the Greek-Syrian era, sports were the result of the influence of Hellenistic culture. Through these games, the Jews became acquainted with the game of ball. This ball of leather was stuffed with sheep's wool inside and is known in classical literature as Pelton.

The essence of the game is to stand a certain distance from one another, and children throw the ball from hand to hand, trying not to let it fall to the ground.

Like the game of ball, they also did exercises near rabbis, especially during the holidays or other special occasions. Rabbi Simon ben Gamaliel (first century) during Sukkot astonished all with his amazing dexterity, throwing simultaneously eight torches into the air. Levi ben Simon did the same thing with eight knives. Rabbi Samuel Flora Emperor performed something similar with eight jugs of wine.

A children's game should be mentioned as one of the most characteristic. A thread was tied to an insect's leg, which moved with the insect until its death, creating an arrangement like a kind of funeral.

The early days of gymnastics are not known. A structure in Jerusalem, the arena, during the Greco-Syrian domination made a large portion of the Jewish people angry. At that time, participation in sports could cause negative reactions among the population. The protest was mainly because of the patronage of the authorities.

Moreover, the high priest Jason—the first to build a similar structure in Jerusalem—could contribute to the popularity of this institution among the wider population of the Jewish people.

Later, Rabbi Simon ben Gamaliel II found it necessary to acquaint five hundred Jewish young people with the basic elements of gymnastics because he found it useful for them. Only Herod the Tsar was engaged in hunting as a sport, as he was addicted to foreign customs. The word "hunter" was so foreign to the Jewish tradition that Amoraim felt it necessary to include a new word in the *agadish* scrolls.

In spite of the harsh ban in some cities in Eastern Europe, it was a custom to play cards for the holiday of Hanukkah in the absence of pecuniary interest. Walking on stilts and playing nuts and balls were permitted for boys and girls.

In Germany, Austria, and Poland, the game of spinning a top with four sides, on which were painted the initials for nothing, half, whole, and cut, would be spun and then added to indicate the result. The origins of the other games went far into the past. They included games with apples, eggs, and balls, as well as "Knight and Robbers," "Caravan of Thieves," "Horse of Abraham," etc. Playing cards spread throughout the fifteenth century. There was evidence that Leon de Modena loved that game very much. In order to prevent the ruination of his reputation because of the spread of the game, an anonymous pamphlet was published, containing information about taking an oath not to play cards for money or other interests.

Some communities, such as Hamburg, Worms, and Bollonskaya, condemned the playing of cards in their rulings. Despite this, great interest occupied students in their spare time. This fact contributed to the hobby of playing cards in a Purim celebration on Sukkot and Chanukah, especially when even the religious scholars and people of science spent their time playing cards.

HANUKKAH GAMES

-

Hanukkah—it is the time of joy and fun games. It is accepted to get together on the first night to sing and make a holiday. The traditional song "Maoz Tzureshuati"—"Strength and rock of my salvation"—glorifies the greatness of God and tells us how God, at all times, kept his people and created wonders for them. Other songs tell of the exploits of Yehuda Maccabi and his brothers, of the miraculous light that drives away the darkness and overcomes all evil, and of a little *sevivon* (dreidel), year after year, pleasing us with its whirling.

Songs were accompanied by dancing and games. Children danced, depicting the Battle of Yehuda Maccabi, spinning like a dreidel, taking up the candle, and converging into one great Hanukkah. There are many Hanukkah songs and games. But, of course, the favorite game of all children is the game of dreidel.

Sevivon is a top with four faces, on each side of which there is a letter in Hebrew written: first *nun*, second *gimel*, third *hey*, and fourth *ne* (if played in Israel) or *bus* (if played outside its boundaries). This is the first letter of the words: Not *gadol haya on* (or *sham*)—a great miracle happened here (or "there").

During the time of Antiochus, Jewish children played with the top. With this game, they disguised and hid the study of the Hebrew alphabet, the Jewish alphabet banned by Greek conquerors.

During Hanukkah, Jews go to visit friends and family or invite them to their houses. On a cold winter evening, when the wind howls outside in the rain or snow, it is accepted to sit together in a warm, elegant, and clean room around the Hanukkah candles twinkling merrily.

There are special Hanukkah treats: potato pancakes (*latkes* or *blintses*) and donuts with jam (*sufgariot*). Both of them are fried in butter and remind us of the miracle of the jug of oil.

JEWS AND SPORTS

-

Historically, Jewish culture has developed a negative attitude toward sporting events. Jews did not take part in the Olympic Games and other sports in ancient times as they were associated with giving sacrifices to the pagan gods. The negative attitude toward sports increased after the Jewish people were under the reign of the Hellenistic Seleucid dynasty, which fostered the cult of the body and sport. In the period of Roman rule, Herod erected a number of sports arenas for gladiatorial sports in the West. But the general attitude toward sports did not change. Attitudes toward sports as a Hellenistic heresy have still been preserved among some ultra-Orthodox Jews.

The attitude of Jews toward sports began to change in the Middle Ages. Maimonides, in particular, promoted the old view that only a healthy body can be home to a healthy heart. In the first half of the twentieth century, among the adherents of this doctrine was the first Ashkenazi Chief Rabbi of the State of Israel, Abraham Isaac Kook.

In the eighteenth century, at the dawn of modern sports, there were famous Jewish athletes. The most famous of them was Dr. Uriel Cymru, according to Daniel Mendoza, a native of Portugal, who was the best fighter in England from 1792 to 1795 and whose fan was the then Prince of Wales. In 1866, the first professional baseball player in the United States was a Jew, Lipman Pike. Canadian Jew Louis Rubenstein won the gold medal at the unofficial world championship of figure skating in 1890.

In 1898, Dr. Max Nordau delivered a speech in Paris about the need for "muscular Judaism" (English muscle Judaism). A Jewish gymnastics club, Bar Kohva (according to Nordau, in response to his call), was established in Berlin the same year. The *Makkabianskoe* movement and Jewish sports associations and clubs have been developed in Palestine and in Europe since 1911.

SPORTS IN CONTEMPORARY ISRAEL

-

Israel has the Israeli Sports Federation, which unites six hundred local clubs (with more than forty thousand members) and sixteen sports, as well as soccer, basketball, tennis...

There are five general sports clubs: Maccabi (thirty local clubs with about forty thousand athletes), Betar, Elitzur, ASA (Students Sports Society), and Shishmon (Tel Aviv) for football clubs.

One of the most significant sporting events held in Israel is the International Maccabiah Games (held every four years; the 16th game was held in 1996) and the game company Hapoel (held every four years; the 16th game was held in 1999).

Israel is a member of the Asian Regional Sports Federation (except for basketball and volleyball, with which Israel has participated in the European Championships).

The largest sports facilities in the country are the following: stadium Ranat-Ghana (with forty thousand seats); Blufeld in Tel Aviv (with twenty-two thousand seats); Kiryat-Elizzer in Haifa (with fourteen thousand seats); as well as stadiums in Netanya and Jerusalem; an athletics sports complex in Josef Hader and the institute named after IO Uigeyta; gymnasiums in Yad-Eliyahu in Tel Aviv, Ramallah, and Haifa; in Molho (Jerusalem), Holon, and Jerusalem in Amkolepo; and a swimming pool in Tel Aviv University.

It is accepted in Israel that the beginning of sports in Eretz Israel started in 1906, the date when in Jaffa and Jerusalem the first gymnastic society was established. The first sports events in Eretz Israel took place in 1908 during the folk festivals in Rehovot.

The beginning of sports activity in Eretz Israel is connected with the name of Elina, who founded the Jerusalem gymnastic society Maccabi (Tel Aviv). In September 1912, the federation Maccabi was founded, and it united two thousand people from twenty local sports clubs. In 1912, in Jerusalem, the first congress of the Maccabi was held. It revealed a reorientation of priorities: the central place, which in Mandatory Palestine belonged to the gym, was given to football.

In 1912, the initiation of young people to sports in the Diaspora established a global alliance of Maccabi. In 1924, it created the sports society Beitar, which was connected with the Zionist movement—the revisionists.

The international arena of Eretz Israel appeared in 1925, when the delegation of the competition of Jewish sports clubs in Vienna arrived at Maccabi.

The central football team of Eretz Israel took part in the qualifying rounds of the World Championships in 1934–1938 (in both cases, it dropped out of the competition after the first round; in 1934, the team lost the game to Egypt twice; and in 1938, it was defeated by the Greece team).

The tense political environment of the late 1930s and The Second World War, and afterward the struggle of the state of Israel for independence, did not contribute to the rapid development of sports in the country. Only the athletes of Eretz Israel in the international arena in those years participated as a part of the united delegations Hapoel and Maccabi in the Festival of Democratic Youth in Prague (1947).

The first championship in the just-declared state of Israel was the country's tennis championship, which was held in 1948. In the same year, the Israeli football team held its first match against the US national team in football. The match ended 3–1 in favor of the United States.

In 1949, Israel's national football team participated in the World Cup, where Yugoslavia lost twice: 6–0 and 5–2. Since then, the Israeli players have regularly taken part in all these championships. The highest achievement was their appearance in the finals in 1970 in Mexico City, when in the final group Israeli footballers defeated New Zealand and Australia, and in the final subgroup they lost to Uruguay (2–0) and had a draw with Sweden (1–1) and Italy (0–0).

Football was the first sport in which a regular national championship was launched in 1950 (except in 1951 and 1953). In 1950, Israel organized the third *Makkabiada*—the first after the Second World War. On the third *Maccabiah*, some delegations were absent from Eastern Europe and Germany.

In 1953, the fourth *Makkabiada* was held. Since then, *Maccabiah* is regularly held every four years, and the International Olympic Committee recognized *Makkabiada* as a regional competition.

In the twelfth Makkabiada, which was held in 1985, there were more than nine thousand athletes from thirty-seven countries.

An important milestone in the history of sports was the foundation of the Olympic Committee in 1951.

Since 1952, Israel has participated in all Olympics. At the Munich Olympics in 1972, eleven members of the Israeli sports delegation were killed by terrorists. In their memory, a tournament in fencing is held annually and a wrestling tournament every two years.

In 1953, Israel founded the student sports association ACA, which has participated regularly in the *Universiades* since 1954. An important event in the history of Israeli sports was the 1957 foundation of the Uigeyta Institute of Physical Culture and Sports.

Nowadays, in Israel, sports competitions among the disabled are widely practiced. The Israeli delegation took an active part in the Olympics in 1986. This competition is regularly held in Israel.

AZERBAIJANI JEWS IN SPORTS

-

In the 1860s of the nineteenth century, Azerbaijan made its first attempts to introduce physical education in schools. In the beginning, it was introduced to the male and female gymnasiums and schools of Baku. Outdoor games were held among schools and preschool children. This is how they were impressed during those games—gymnastic society member M. M. Ryzhanskaya remembers: "During the games, a very ragged Jewish boy of thirteen watched the game, then threw his balloon and ran up to the players. The teacher leading the game offered him a book. A smile of joy spread over the face of the child. The turn of passing on the baton fell on the good-looking and neatly dressed eleven-year-old boy. Running around the circle, the boy looked for someone to select his comrade. Suddenly, he stopped behind a ragged boy and hit his back twice. If only you could see the facial expressions of a crocked man. Suddenly, the boy guessed that he was selected. The boy ran away to meet his new friend. He pressed him so that it seemed he choked with delight. He looked around, his eyes were calling all who admired him. He was happy to show how he was selected, embraced, and accepted as an equal with them."

The development of modern sports in Azerbaijan started at the end of the nineteenth century. It was due to the desire of the Azerbaijani and Russian bourgeoisie to use sports for the physical development and education of young people in their class and to strengthen their dominant generation. Particular preference was given to gymnastics, tennis, fencing, swimming, sailing, and rowing. In this regard, there were sports clubs and societies in Baku that united the aristocratic youth of the city. In 1926, special attention was given to intensifying the work on the development of boxing in Azerbaijan. Thanks to the visits and performances of Baku boxers and coaches in cities and regions of the country, the number of supporters of this sport culture increased. In 1929, the first match between Baku and Rostov boxers was held in Baku. The growth of the skills of Azerbaijani boxers in 1928–1929 was the result of the professional development of the coaching staff. The visit of A. Holstein, the national champion, to Baku was of particular importance. Under his leadership, the technique and tactics of such athletes of the DSO "Dynamo" as N. Kitasov, A. Baryshev, A. Nechaev and others improved significantly. This allowed some of them to achieve the honorary titles of champions and prize winners of the USSR championships.

In 1929, there was a competition among Caucasian athletes in weight lifting. Their program included lifting, weight lifting, wrestling, and boxing. Azerbaijani boxers came out on top.

At the beginning of 1930, some team meetings were held between the boxers of Baku, Tbilisi, and Rostov. In August, boxers' trade union workers met with the team of the Moscow trade union organization; the athletes of Baku won the game, 5–1.

A big stadium with a good gym was built in Baku in 1926. The quality of sports facilities improved. There was a positive impact on the sport of gymnastics in the 1928 All Union Olympic gymnastics competition, which took place in 1928, where Iskinsky K. and A. Sokhatsky took first place.

Until 1925, weight lifting in Azerbaijan had been developing too slowly compared with other sports. This is explained mainly by the fact that weight training sessions required special facilities, sports equipment, and coaching staff.

The winners of the championship of the republic in 1926 due to weight categories were A. Schultz, W. Unikin, I. Merkuris, and G. Dick. Since then, competition in the weight lifting championships of the republic has become an annual event. In 1927, in Tbilisi, the Transcaucasian championship in weight lifting was held. A. Schultz took second place in this championship.

The views on individual types of sports gradually changed. The slogan "Only Records!" found a live response among Azerbaijani weight lifters.

In 1931–1932, Azerbaijani weight lifters were already considered the strongest among the Transcaucasian republics. In these years, Azerbaijani weight lifters achieved not only Caucasian but all-Union records. These included the champions of the Soviet Union in 1931, A. Schultz and G. Bromberg.

The second all-Azerbaijani Olympics was a tangible incentive to the development of physical culture and sports among women in Azerbaijan. The finals of the Olympics preceded a sports festival that was held in two hundred physical culture collectives of different enterprises, factories, and schools. About eight hundred female athletes attended these competitions. This list includes, first of all, a record-holder in athletics, Ms. Urbanowich.

The most significant sports event of 1933 was the primacy of the Central Council of Dynamo in athletics, which was held from the twenty-first to the twenty-third of September in Baku. The championship was attended by over four hundred of the best athletes in society. Azerbaijani sportsmen won the third prize. Many of them set new Caucasian records. These included the results of the women's 100 meters, G. Peterson (12, 9); the relay race (4 x 100 m women), G. Urbanovich and G. Peterson (54.4); throwing grenades, G. Urbanovich (35, 10), the core (9 m 81), height (138.5), etc.

The new rise of sport—technical indicators of Azerbaijani athletes in 1935 were marked during the year, which improved the records of the republic, the Caucasus, and the Soviet Union.

Since 1934, Azerbaijani weight lifters have successfully participated in match competitions with athletes from other cities in the Soviet Union.

In 1934, a great sports event—the first all-Azerbaijan weight lifting competition—was held, where, along with new Azerbaijani weight lifters, athletes from Moscow also took an active part. Great success in these competitions was made by I. Bromberg, a sailor (Baku). Participating as a flyweight champion, he set a new right-handed record for Azerbaijan (48.5), which exceeded the all-Union record of 2 kg.

As it is seen, in only one year, Azerbaijani weight lifters improved eight records in the republic, one in the Union, and one in the Transcaucasian. Great success fell on the lot of another weight lifter—A. Schultz. Participating in the 1935 USSR weight lifting championship, he set a new record in the bench press (with both hands) of 101.2 kg. (average weight) In addition to our other weight lifter Schulz, I. Bromberg set eight new Transcaucasian records.

In 1933–1937, the subject of gymnastics and its role in the system of physical education were defined. Relatively independent types of gymnastics were determined: the main gymnastics, sports, artistic acrobatics, hygienic, and medical gymnastics at work. Special popularity belonged to gymnastics. The professional skills of gymnasts were growing everywhere. In those years, all-Union competitions became the start of a systematic process. In 1933, the first Caucasian gymnastics preliminary was held in Tiflis to participate in the championship of the

USSR. Some women gymnasts, like K. Vorovich and N. Butz from Azerbaijan participated in these competitions. Since that year, Azerbaijani gymnasts have begun to take part in all-Union competitions.

The years 1933–1937 were the period of significant development of sports games in Azerbaijan. Volleyball became one of the most popular games in Azerbaijan. It attracted not only the young but also adults. Volleyball rapidly spread not only in the cities but also in the countryside.

THE JEWS DO NOT KILL

-

In fact, this event is not a fantasy or an invention of the author. While visiting one of the synagogues in the city of Baku, I managed to have a conversation with a ninety-year-old rabbi about the sports life of the Jews in Baku and their role in sports in general. After all, the synagogue is not only a house of prayer but also a place for noble news. That's what the Rabbi remembered. The geologist Razdolsky, a Jew by nationality, went on a sport hunt with a camera in the 1950s.

A shot rang out, and after that, a man jumped down from the tree.

"If you took a bit further to the right, I would get all the charge on my back."

"Who would believe that there was a man in the tree but not a pheasant?"

"You have to be careful…To my luck—it was a bad, bad shooting."

"And are you better?"

"Better."

"Where are the weapons?"

"That's it!"

And the man who jumped from the tree put a leather case on an eye-watering "FED."

"One! Done. Now you can't leave me."

They both laughed and shook hands.

"Agronomist Stepanov!"

"Geologist Razdolsky!"

"I am practicing shooting," said Stepanov.

"I consider it to be an unworthy occupation for a civilized man to shoot aimlessly at the game. I usually hunt with a camera, and it's much more interesting," Razdolsky said.

He sat on the hemp smoke. Razdolsky pulled out his wallet and a stack of pictures.

"Here is my prey! I tracked down birds' nests, dens of beasts, and masks and tried to shoot at the different moments of their lives. It's fun and an exciting sport. Look how the black grouse expresses his love of his beloved, and a fox gets out of the foxhole and makes his morning toilet, but…this was an interesting case while hunting gazelle. I was lying in the reeds beside the path, along which gazelles go to the water, holding their devices at the ready.

"A small group of gazelles peacefully moved on a broad plain closer to me, and I survived when they came closer so I could take their pictures. Suddenly, I noticed the footsteps of another hunter at 250 steps. It was a young wolf. It also hunted and was sprawled on the ground, waiting for the approximation of gazelles. I took the binoculars and watched the wolf. One of the gazelles, fighting off competition from the herd, went toward the wolf. The wolf followed it with greedy eyes, measured the distance impatiently, and jumped with his back legs. Suddenly, the wolf jumped with a desperate leap but failed. The herd of gazelles, in the blink of an eye, started running at gallop, raising a cloud of dust. The wolf, running past me in pursuit, soon realized his mistake: he did not have endurance anymore, and he jumped too early. I took him in when he confused his tail and turned back, making sure that I had made a mistake in the calculation."

At the end of the story, I had to clarify some details of this event. I came to the conclusion that, according to the Rabbi, who with what pain told this case, millions of Jews were killed in various concentration camps, and among them, of course, there were quite a few Jewish athletes. I'm searching for the names and details of the dead athletes for the next edition.

The rabbi told it based on the sixth commandment of the Torah.

"Don't kill"

ATHLETICS

-

Galina Ganeker (born April 10, 1917, Baku) is a Soviet athlete, an honored master of sports of the USSR (1943), and an advocate of Baku sports clubs Bolshevik, Neftyanik (1934–1947), and Leningrad–SKA (1948–1953).

She was an under-bronze medalist in 1950 and the six-time champion of the USSR (1939–1948) in the high jump, and the result, with whom she became a champion of the USSR in 1948 (1.63 m), would be enough to win the bronze medal at the Olympic Games in 1948.

Ganeker, first Soviet high jump world level: the

results of the top ten results of the season in the world in 1940, 1943–1945 (1945, leader of the season), 1947–1952. In 1939–1945, she was the undisputed leader of the USSR. In 1946, leadership passed to Alexander Chudinov. After a season in 1947, Ganeker moved to Leningrad, where she began to train Gregory Nikiforov, and in 1948 she was able to win the USSR Chudinov championship (1.63 m vs. 1.60 m).

The Second World War, Ganeker worked in the hospital as a nurse.

Olympics		
High Jump		
	Place	Result
1952	11th	1.55 meters
European Championship		
1950	3rd	1.63 meters
USSR Championship		
1936	2nd	1,50 meters
1937	2nd	1,50 meters
1938		
1939	Champion	1,55 meters
1940	Champion	1,55 meters
1943	Champion	1,55 meters
1944	Champion	1,55 meters
1945	Champion	1,55 meters
1946		
1947	2nd	1,60 meters
1948	Champion	1,63 meters
1949	2nd	1,57 meters
1950	2nd	1,58 meters
1951	2nd	1,61 meters
1952	3rd	1,58 meters

Well-Known Sportswoman of Azerbaijan

Galina Ganeker came into sports in 1932. At the very first lessons in gymnastics in the alliance Medsantrud, she was noticed for her persistence and great natural jumping ability. Arriving at the stadium, she eagerly became involved, literally, in all kinds of athletics.

Persistent training, combined with good physical qualities, enabled her to become one of the best jumpers in the Soviet Union in three years' time.

Galina Ganeker's success was not reflected in her studies at AKII, where she was a third-year student.

During the 1936 sports season, Azerbaijani athletes successfully participated in many competitions. In the person-team primacy of the Soviet Union, G. Ganiker, a girl from Baku, achieved good results in the high jump (1 m, 50 cm) and in the race with hurdles at 80 m (12.5 s). The results were the best in the former USSR.

In all-Union competitions in 1937 in athletics, Galina took 156 cm of height by setting the new all-Union achievement, breaking the old, eight-year-old record that belonged to Shamanov, an honored master of sports (Moscow).

Galina Ganeker—Athlete of All-Union Category

Women

Introduction of uniform standards for all-Union athletics classification of athletes was determined by categories. According to the classification of the all-Union athletes in Baku, only two athletes belong to the first section. One of them is Galina Ganeker.

Zakavkazy Record		
	Running	
	Length	Result
G. Peterson	60 meters	8 s
G. Peterson	100 meters	12.9 s
G. Ganeker	400meters (baryer)	1.10,003sec.
G. Ganeker	60 meters (baryer)	9.8 s

Republican Championship in Athletics

In the running jump, the master of the sport, Ganeker, was the first with a score of 4 m, 86 cm.

For women running with barriers at 80 m, Ganeker was the first, as expected, with 13.8 sec. A master of sports, Galina Ganeker won the event (triathlon), gaining 1,443 points. From the technical superiority of the results, it should be noted that the achievements of master of sports Galina Ganeker (Akii), who jumped 5 m, 25 cm in length, thereby setting a new record for Azerbaijan, fulfilled the norm of master in the sport.

The new rise of sports—the technical performance of athletes of the Azerbaijan SSR in 1935, which was marked during the year—improved the records of the republic, the Caucasus, and the Soviet Union.

Galina Urbanovich
(September 5, 1917, Baku–May
8, 2011)
Soviet gymnast, Olympic cham-
pion in 1952
Honored master of sports
Honored coach of the RSFSR.

Olympics		
Gold	Helsinki 1952	Team championship
Silver	Helsinki 1952	Group exercise
Championship USSR		
Gold	1939	Gold
Silver	1939	Floor exercise
Bronze	1939	All around
Bronze	1939	Crossbar
Gold	1943	Absolute championship
Gold	1943	Vault
Gold	1943	Horse

Silver	1943	Bars
Silver	1943	Ring
Silver	1943	Crossbar
Gold	1944	Absolute championship
Gold	1944	Bars
Gold	1944	Horse
Gold	1944	Ring
Silver	1944	Vault
Silver	1944	Floor exercise
Gold	1945	Absolute championship
Gold	1945	Horse
Silver	1945	Vault
Silver	1945	Ring
Silver	1945	Crossbar
Bronze	1945	Bars
Gold	1946	Absolute championship
Gold	1946	Bars
Gold	1946	Ring
Gold	1946	Floor exercise

Silver	1946	Vault
Silver	1946	Crossbar
Gold	1947	Absolute championship
Gold	1947	Beam
Gold	1948	Absolute championship
Gold	1948	Vault
Gold	1948	Bars
Gold	1948	Ring
Gold	1948	Crossbar
Gold	1947	Beam
Bronze	1947	Vault
Gold	1949	Bars
Gold	1949	Ring
Silver	1949	All around
Silver	1949	Vault
Silver	1949	Crossbar
Gold	1950	Absolute championship
Gold	1950	Bars
Gold	1950	Ring

Silver	1950	Beam
Silver	1951	All around
Silver	1951	Bars
Gold	1952	Ring
Gold	1952	Floor exercise
Silver	1953	All around
Silver	1953	Ring

Hostage of the Great Patriotic War

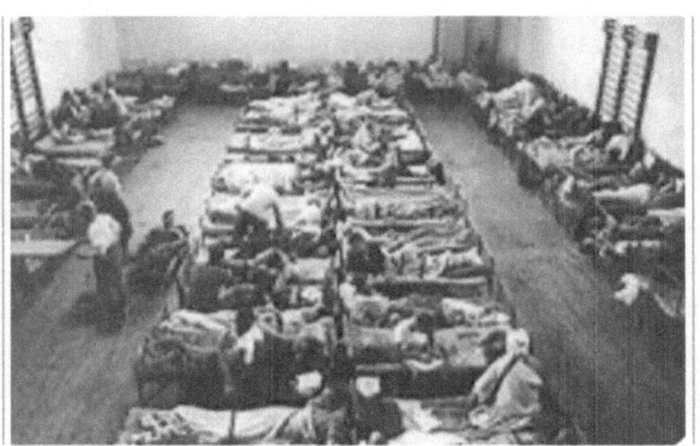

G. Urbanovich worked as a patronage nurse,
caring for the sick and wounded.

Galina Urbanovich is an honored coach of the RSFSR, an honored master of sports of the USSR, an Olympic champion, a seven-time absolute champion of the USSR, a twenty-two-time champion of the USSR in certain types of all-around events, and a judge in the international category.

The war slowed down the rapid career of a talented athlete. At first, she had no time for training at all as she worked as a patronage nurse and cared for the sick and wounded. However, when the opportunity arose, Galina returned to the gym. Even during the war, it was possible, at the very least, to establish the sports life of the country, and in 1943, the athlete, who was in her prime, achieved an impressive success—she became the absolute champion of the Soviet Union. Months passed, the roar of exploding shells gradually subsided, and Galina Urbanovich's fame only grew. At domestic competitions, she did not give her rivals a single chance and therefore became the absolute champion of the country seven times.

Valery Vladimirovich Belenky (born September 5, 1969, in Baku) is a Soviet, Azerbaijani, and German gymnast of Jewish origin, an Olympic champion in 1992, a three-time world champion, and an honored master of sports in the USSR. At the 1992 Olympic Games, he played for the United Team, representing Azerbaijan.

Due to the fact that Azerbaijan did not have its own gymnastics federation, in 1993, at the World Championships in Birmingham, Belenky performed as an athlete not registered for any country and took a bronze medal in exercises on uneven bars.

He has been living in Germany since 1994. He played for the German national team at the 1996 Olympics. Since 2009, together with the honored coach of the USSR, Anatoly Yarmovsky, he has coached Shakir Shikhaliyev, who represented Azerbaijan at the 2012 Summer Olympics in London.

The tireless Maria Urbanowich pleased all in javelin throwing. Combining a new red spurt with an elastic jerk, she broke her previous record of 29 m, 1 cm, throwing a spear at 30 m, 8 cm.

Setting New Records

Urbanowich, among women, did not reach a record of one hundred meters for only one second in the sprint. She demonstrated much higher results than the record results of Azerbaijan during the training several times.

"I hoped to set a record in grenade throwing. I wish that these events were more organized and without the judicial incidents that happened last year."

Urbanowich Tear the Tape First

Maria Urbanowich (Dynamo) showed the best results in the run at 100 m at 13.1 s.

T. N. Dmitrashvili was nominated as a candidate for the position of member of the Dzerzhinsky District Council. The general meeting of the academy collaborators, students, workers, and employees of the Azerbaijan Industrial Institute, named after Azimbekova, discussed the issue  of nominating candidates for Dzerzhinsky District Council and decided: "Nominate the candidacy of Tamara Dimtrashvili, fifth year student of the energy department, for Dzerzhinsky District Council on 187 constituency. Tamara Dmitrashvili participating in DSO Oilman this year for her high achievements in sports has won the right to receive the rank of master in athletics."

Republican Competitions on Athletics, Day of the Relays

On October 1, the republican athletics championship started in the stadium Dynamo. The number of participants reached five hundred. Bad weather forced the event to be moved to the evening. By five o'clock, the participants had lined up. They came out onto the field to the melody of the march.

In the 4 x 400 relay race among the women, the struggle was only on the first step. T. Dmitriashvili ("Neftyanik"), who passed the second stage well, broke away from the team Az. SIFCO 10–12 m; by the end of the competition, this clearance distance had reached 20 m, and the Oilers finished first with a time of 54.4 seconds, repeating an Azerbaijani record.

Azerbaijan New Records

The performances of Baku athletes attracted great interest in sports. The start of the competition gathered the strongest runners in Baku: Ostrovsky, Safarov, Orujov, Bergen, and others. In the first kilometer, Ostrovsky was ahead of all, but being unable to distribute his power properly, he lost his breath and left the track. Having run out the distance, Bergen from Dynamo came up to reach the line first, with a good result of 11 m, 1 s.

Five Best Athletes

The year 1939 was marked by new achievements by Azerbaijani athletes. Here are the best track and field athletes for certain types of athletics and the results compared with 1938.

Again, T. Dmitrashvili pleased all in the women's 800 meters. With almost masculine steps, she went ahead without much stress from all and first touched the ribbon with a new record of Az. SSR, showing 3 m, 32.3 s.

Running in 100 meters

Women

1. G. Urbanowich–12.8 (Dynamo)
2. T. Dmitrashvili–13.0 (Neftyanik)

Running in 200 meters

Women

1. G. Urbanowicz–27, 6 (Dynamo)
2. T. Dmitrashvili–28.8 (Neftyanik)

Running in 1,500 meters

Men

1. Bergen—4:32,2 (Dynamo)

Competition in the 4 x 100 Relay

On November 12, at the Lenin stadium, competitions were held among the collectives of sports societies Dynamo and Neftyanik in the 4 x 100 relay race for the prize of the Baku Committee for Physical Culture and Sports. The girls were the first to begin the race.

AUTO MOTOR SPORT

-

An auto motor competition for the individual championship of Azerbaijan took place on Saray Highway on August 18, 20–21.

The program of events included the following distances: one mile from the course, 100 km, and a 20-km cross-country race.

Zinkovsky, Roginsky, the best riders of Azerbaijan took an active part in this competition.

The participants of the auto moto rally along the regions of Azerbaijan on the road. Athlete Sivitskaya on a motorcycle.

BASKETBALL

-

It is not only a coincidence that in 1926 there were nearly three hundred basketball teams in Baku. In addition, the number of people engaged in basketball increased not only in the capital but also in the regions. As the number of basketball teams

increased, their technical and tactical qualities also improved. Since 1923, the basketball programs have been included in all the competitions, including those of 1920–1930. At that time, a strong basketball team was formed at the Iron Road sports club. The selected team became a national champion for several years. The role of Q. Abramov, Y. Arunov, and I. Ionov was great in the development of the team. Additionally, thanks to experienced specialists, the popularity of this game has spread more widely in our country. Since 1930, the republic has had the right to participate in the Caucasus and USSR championships. Our selected basketball team, which participated in the first group of the USSR championship in 1936, won the Georgian team at 41:20, the Belorussian National team at 30:16, the Kharkov city team (the Ukraine) at 23:3, the Sverdlovsk (Russia) team at 28:14, the team of Kiev at 25:17, and finally took third place in the championship.

Baku Championship in Basketball

The sports hall Dynamo held a championship where a basketball match between the teams Neftyanik and Dynamo (Baku) met. In the second half, the fifth player of Dynamo, Azbil, proved to be the best. After a hard struggle, the Dynamo equalized the score and brought it to a 32:23 victory.

A talented player, Abramashvili, also played as part of Dynamo.

BILLIARDS

-

On April 15, 1939, Dynamo held a billiard competition among the sportsmen in the sports society.
Kreis won the first place.

BOXING

-

Competition Boxers

One hundred and five boxers took part in the boxing competitions. The evening opened with a match of flyweight boxers.

In the ring, Bogdanov (Leningrad) performed strong and decisive attacks, while Wittenberg (Baku) easily avoided the attacks, stepped aside, and made the Leningrader lose balance and hang on the ropes. Wittenberg used these moments to score points. In the third round, he worked boldly and won the round and the match.

Young Bakuvian lightweight Mass vigorously resisted against Moscovite Ivanov, but the experienced master Ivanov won the competition. Mass's other opponent was Petrov, the Leningrader. The match wasn't so bright. Only Mass had the advantage and won the match.

Boxing Matches of Baku and Grozny Boxers

The Central Committee of the Union of Oil Fields of the Caucasus in boxing held a championship in Grozny on May 27.

The meeting began with a huge crowd of spectators in the summer theater of old crafts. Flyweight Krintsman (Baku) easily achieved a real advantage over Egorov (Grozny) in the first round.

Chelninsky, a lightweight boxer (Baku), cleverly fought against the temperamental Veyntsela (Grozny). The Baku boxer repelled all attacks by Veyntsela with an extraordinary sense of distance and put him in a very difficult position. In the middle of the first round, he ended the fight with a knockout of Veyntselem.

The unexpected ability was demonstrated by seventeen-year-old heavyweight (90 kg) Goygov (Grozny) in a fight against Berkman (Baku). Moving with surprising lightness, he easily exchanged blows. Despite the two knockdowns in the first round and boldly proposing an active fight in the second round, he himself fell to a knockout. Despite all this, it happened so that he remained the best fighter on the Grozny team.

1.   Goldstein Alexander Alexandrovich

A. Goldstein, a well-known sportsman and honored master of sports, gained the title of USSR champion in 1926 and 1927. He was sent to Baku from Moscow as a trainer by the sports society Dynamo, and as a trainer, he has played a great role in the development of the sports skills and abilities of Azerbaijani boxers.

He has managed the boxing department in Dynamo for about ten years and brought up a number of boxing masters. N. Kitasov, A. Barishev, L. Saplivenko, the winners and medalists of the USSR championships, and others were among them.

2.   Dobrinskiy Lev Georgiyevich

He was born in Baku on September 28, 1929. He got his secondary education at the school for

deaf and dumb children. His trainer was Alexander Kruchkov. Afterward, he developed his sports mastership under the leadership of Ilya Godunov, the honored trainer in the Burevestnik sports society. He was a quintuple Azerbaijan champion, won the championship held by the Central Council of the USSR Trade Unions, and took fourth place in the USSR championship in 1953–1954. Has won 183 out of 198 in the ring. He is a USSR sports master.

3.   Odinov Ilya Lvovich

He was born on April 12, 1917. He graduated from the Azerbaijan State University of Physical Education and the Azerbaijan State Oil and Gas University. He worked for the sports societies Burevestnik and reserve labor forces as a boxing coach. Afterward, he worked as a senior lecturer at the department of weight lifting and boxing at the State Institute of Physical Culture for many years. He has made

great efforts to bring up skilled personnel and high-level athletes.

His pupils, V. Odinov, V. Kipiani, V. Golubenko, V. Filippenko, Y. Sekasov, T. Babanli, L. Dobrinskiy, A. Salmanov, A. Acalov, and many others, have been champions and medalists in USSR and international competitions.

There are dozens of associate professors, professors, and honorary coaches among Ilya Lvovich's pupils.

Ilya Odinov is one of the founders of the boxing school. He has been a champion of Azerbaijan several times, the winner of all-Union competitions, and a medalist in the USSR championship.

Due to his high sports performance, the USSR sports master, the referee of the Soviet Union category, was awarded the title of honorary coach of the USSR. After a serious illness, he passed away forever in Moscow in 1987.

4.   Ibrahim Ashumov

He is one of the pioneers of boxing. Having good techniques and a strong blow, Ashumov successfully participated in many all-Union and international competitions and made his fans happy. He

won a silver medal in the USSR championship in 1937. In the same year, he was awarded the title of master of sports. He was also a participant in the Great Patriotic War. He spent the last years of his life in Moscow.

5.   Boris Semyonovich Sxirasvili

He was born in Baku on July 23, 1936. He has been engaged in boxing under A. Kryuckov's leadership in Dynamo since 1953.

He became the winner of the Baku and Soviet Union championships in 1958. The central council of Dynamo was the winner in the USSR championship and silver medalist in regional competition.

He graduated from the State Institute of Physical Culture. He was a trainer, an instructor, and the chief of the department in the Neftchik sport society for many years.

He has been awarded the titles of master of sports of the USSR and international referee (AIBA).

In 1961, he moved to the Kazakhstan State Sports Committee and worked in a number of administrative posts. He successfully fulfilled the duty of referee in the world, at the Asian championships, and at the Olympics.

CHESS AND CHECKERS

-

Chess and Checkers Tournament of Scientists

Leonid Listengarten

Leonid Borisovich Listinggarten (born 1935, Baku) is an Azerbaijani chess player, master of sports in the USSR (1961), and doctor of technical sciences.

I became interested in chess in the fourth grade, successfully performed in the championships of the Azerbaijan SSR in 1955 (1–2) and 1960 (2 places), and played for Neftchik (Baku).

Listengarten teaches classes at a Jewish
school (Orlando, Florida, 2005).

He graduated from the Faculty of Geology at the Azerbaijan Industrial Institute and received the title of engineer-geologist. He worked as the head of the department for the development of oil and gas fields at the design institutes Aznipinef and Gipromorneft, where he led the design and analysis of the development of offshore fields in the Caspian Sea. He lives in the USA. He teaches at a Jewish school in Orlando, Florida.

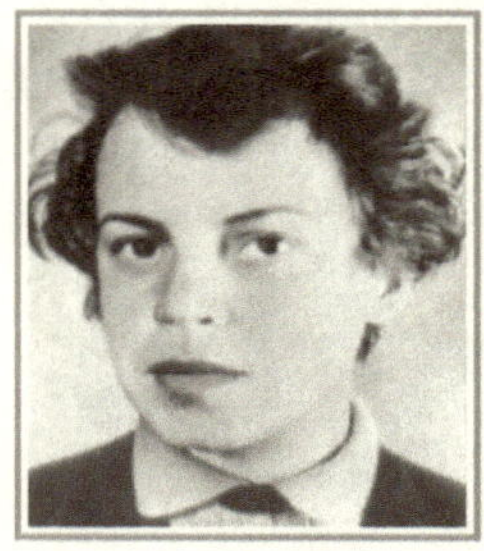

Zatulovskaya Tatyana Yakovlevna (December 8, 1935, Baku, Azerbaijan Republic–July 2, 2017, Ashkelon, Israel) was a Soviet-later Israeli chess player and engineer-geologist. She was a grandmaster (1976) and an honored master of sports in the USSR (1967).

Her first coach was Azer Zeynalli, who was several years older than her. Since 1947, she has studied in the chess circle of the Baku House of Pioneers. She graduated from the Faculty of Geology of the Azerbaijan Industrial Institute with a degree in engineer-geology. In 1973, having married (her second marriage) to football observer Valery Vinokurov, she moved to Moscow.

She was a winner and prizewinner of many international competitions and championships of the USSR (1960, 1962, 1963), a contender for the title of world champion (1961, 1964, 1967), and, as part of the USSR national team, the winner of two Olympics (1963 and 1966).

Since 1967, she has been an honored master of sports in the USSR. She was a five-time champion of the Burevestnik sports society.

Since 2001, she has lived in Ashkelon (Israel).

In her last years, Tanya lived in Israel, on the Mediterranean coast. Tanya loved to swim. As always, on July 2 of this year, in the morning, she went to the seashore with her female companion. But very soon, one of her friends suddenly noticed Tanya lying lifeless in the water right by the shore. Death came to her instantly.

Alexander Rosenthal was born in Baku in 1967 to Jewish parents—a pediatrician mother and an engineer father. He learned how to play chess at the age of six by watching his uncle and cousin's chess battles. When his mother took him to a chess coach, the coach first refused to accept him because of his young age, but she insisted, and after winning a few games against older children, the coach gave in. He was a Baku champion in all three youth age categories—U9, U12, and U16. He took part in his first adult republic chess championship at the age of seven. He was too short to reach the board and had to ask the organizers to put books on top of the chair to see it.

He was the captain of his school chess team in the White Rook USSR youth competition in 1980, an Azerbaijan U18 chess champion in 1984, the captain of the Azerbaijan team in the Youth Spartakiad of the USSR in 1984 in Tashkent, a member of the Azerbaijan team in the 1985 Spartakiad of Peoples of the USSR in Volgograd, and a Baku chess champion in 1987.

He graduated from Azerbaijan State University with a major in applied mathematics. In 1991, he moved to the USA. Since 1995, he has been working for the US government at the National Institutes of Health (NIH). He has been working at the Chief Technology Office for the National Institute of Allergy and Infectious Diseases at NIH since 2013. He authored over forty scientific papers and received over fifty professional awards, including two highly prestigious presidential rank awards—in 2017 (from President Trump) and in 2022 (from President Biden).

Shur Michale is a master of sports in the USSR and a master of sports in international class. He was born in Baku, Azerbaijan, in 1962. He graduated from the energy department of the Azerbaijan Oil Academy in 1983.

From 1987 to 1997, he worked as the head of the financial and economic department in the system of the Ministry of Energy of the Republic of Azerbaijan. From 1997 to 2002, he was the head of cultural and sports programs at the Baku JCC. From 1998 to 2000, he was a presenter of the chess section of the central newspaper *Vyshka* in Baku. From 2000 to 2002, he was the deputy general director of Maccabi in Azerbaijan. From 2001 to 2002, he was the head of the business school at the Embassy of Israel in the Republic of Azerbaijan.

He was a three-time champion of Azerbaijan among youth, a two-time winner of the Azerbaijan Cup, a two-time vice champion of the USSR among youth, a bronze medalist of the USSR team championship, and a vice champion of the 15th World Maccabiah (Israel, Jerusalem, 2001).

He has been a coach since 1985. He trained seven international grandmasters and national and international masters. Together with his students, he won the titles of world and European champions among youth and champions of Azerbaijan and the State of Massachusetts. He worked as a trainer in Azerbaijan, Russia, the Czech Republic, Israel, and the USA. From 2003 to 2004, he was the head coach and tournament director of the Springfield Chess Club, MA. From 2004 to 2007, he was the head chess coach at Schoolplus, a private school in Northampton. From 2007 to present, he is the director of the cultural, educational, and sports programs of Serenity Care in Springfield, Massachusetts. He is the trainer of leading chess players in Massachusetts.

Korsunsky Rostislav Rostislavovich was born on February 18, 1957, in a Jewish family in the city of Baku, Azerbaijan. He was a master of sports in international class. From an early age, the passion for chess led the young Rostislav Korsunsky to the then-famous House of Pioneers in Baku.

In a short time, he mastered the rules of chess. He became a five-time champion of Azerbaijan, a member of the Azerbaijan chess team, and a partic-ipant and winner of prestigious international tour-naments. The bloody events in Baku on January 20, 1990—the murder of innocent children and women by the Soviet army—had a strong influence on R. Korsunsky.

Talented master Korsunsky with young Garry Kasparov

He was the champion of Azerbaijan in 1980, 1983, 1985, 1989, and 1990. According to eyewitnesses from that period, he died near his house, next to garbage cans, in 1996. He was buried at the Jewish cemetery in Baku. Grandmaster Garry Kasparov lived next door. According to Baku chess coaches, R. Korsunsky brought G. (then Weinstein) Kasparov to the chess class of the House of Pioneers. In the photo, young Garry Kasparov is next to the talented master R. Korsunsky. In the house where our hero grew up, there was a famous park in Baku named after the legendary intelligence officer of the Second World War, Richard Sorg, who was born in Baku.

Pavlenko Oleg was born in 1942 in Tashkent.

When he was six years old, he began to play chess in Voronezh. In 1950, he moved to the city of Baku and entered the House of Pioneers chess club.

In 1956, he became the first champion of Azerbaijan among boys and executed the norm of MMR (candidate master). In 1957, 1958, 1959, and 1960, he confirmed the title, becoming the champion of Azerbaijan among young men.

In May 1961, in Belgrade, he participated in the youth team of the USSR against the national team of Yugoslavia and played with Parma (0.5: 1.5), Velimirovic (1:0), and Kavalevich (0.5: 0.5).

In August 1961, in Lviv, Pavlenko took third place in an international youth tournament. The first place went to V. Savon, and the second place went to

Kuinji. We were ahead of Jansa, Yanatu, and other foreign players. The coach in Lviv was unforgettable: Sultan Khalilbeyli.

In 1961, the tournament was held in Moscow for Moscow's strongest young men up to twenty years old, where he took first place. The coach was then Ch.A. Sultanov, who was instrumental in the opening preparations.

He was a three-time champion in Baku among men: in 1962 and 1964, and the last time Pavlenko became the champion of Baku was in 2003.

In 1965, he graduated from the IPA them. VI Lenin (now the University of Tusi), specializing as a teacher of mathematics and physics.

Back in 1966, in the national championship, Dynamo took second place and executed the norm of master of sports in the USSR chess.

In 1967, he participated in the national championship for men in Kharkiv and scored 7 points out of 13 (51 among 130 participants).

From 1968 to 1973, he was the champion of the Baku Air Defense District. In 1968 and 1970, he became the champion of Azerbaijan among men. Since 1992, he has been the head coach of the Nasimi chess school. Since 1997, he has become a FIDE master in chess.

Pavlenko prepared grandmasters Azer Mirzoyev, Rasul Ibragimov, Rashad Babayev, CMC-Zaur Mammadov, Nurlana Mehbalieva, and Idrisov Tabriz. He occasionally worked with Teimour Radjabov, Rauf Mammadov, and Gadyr Huseynov, assisted by A. Sofiev.

Garry began regular chess lessons at the Baku Palace of Pioneers at the age of seven. Master Oleg Isaakovich Privorotsky became his first coach. At the same age, he lost his father, who died of lymphosarcoma. In 1975, when Garry was twelve, his mother changed her father's surname from Weinstein to Kasparov. This was done with the consent of relatives in order to facilitate the further chess career of a young but already promising chess player, which could be prevented by the anti-Semitism that existed in the USSR.

Garry Kimovich Kasparov (surname at birth was Weinstein; born April 13, 1963 in Baku, Azerbaijan, SSR, USSR) is a Soviet and Russian chess player, the 13th world chess champion, a chess writer, and a politician who has been repeatedly recognized as the greatest chess player in history. He became an international grandmaster (1980), an honored master of sports in the USSR (1985), a champion in the USSR (1981, 1988), and a champion in Russia (2004).

He is an eight-time winner in the World Chess Olympiads: four times in the USSR team (1980, 1982, 1986, 1988) and four times in the Russian team (1992, 1994, 1996, 2002). He is a winner of eleven chess "Oscars" (prizes for the best chess player of the year). Kasparov single-handedly headed the FIDE rating from 1985 to 2006 with two short breaks; in 1994, he was excluded from the rating by a FIDE decision adopted in 1993. In 1999, Garry Kasparov reached a record rating of 2,851 points. The record stood for thirteen and a half years until it was broken by Magnus Carlsen.

Teymur bears his mother's surname.

Teymur Rajabov was born in Baku, Azerbaijan, on March 12, 1987. His father, Boris Efimovich Sheinin, is a Jew by origin. As a child, he lived next door to Garry Kasparov and went to the same chess club with him.

He was an Azerbaijani chess player, a grandmaster (2001), a semifinalist in the 2004 World Championship, a three-time European champion (2009, 2013, 2017) of the team championship as part of the Azerbaijani team, and a World Cup Winner (2019).

Two Credits for the Title of Candidate Master

Baku draughts player of the first category of the USSR, Zelikman D. A. was awarded two points for his success in previous Union competitions for the title of candidate master in the USSR.

Chess and Checkers School

Systematic studies on advanced training for chess and checkers players in the I–II categories were organized for a number of years. Well-known

Azerbaijani sportsmen Doktorskiy and Zelikman were invited as consultants.

Chess and Checkers Semifinals

In the semifinals of the Baku chess and checkers championship, the competition became harder and harder with each round.

Rosenblatt played a better game against Barinov, but having an easy win in the endgame, he made a mistake and made it possible for Barinov to finish the game in a draw. In the previous game, Rosenblatt, playing with blacks against Osipova, methodically beat the enemy and forced him to surrender.

In the chess semifinals, Doktorskiy defeated Sienkievich.

Chess Tournament Neftyanik

The chess tournament of the sport society Neftyanik came to an end in Baku. Thirteen players took part in the final part. The first place in the tournament was taken by Gegelgants, and the fourth place was taken by Krintsman.

Chess Tournament for the Baku Championship

Another chess championship started in Baku. For the best chess player title, fourteen people—the strongest I category players of Baku—competed in this championship. Among them was the winner of the qualifying tournaments—Doktorskiy.

Women's Chess School

On September 30, 1938, Baku Women's Chess School started at the chess-checkers club. There was no need to speak about the appropriateness and necessity of this school. The fact that our female players needed systematic study was clear to everyone.

One of the objectives of opening a school is to impart the correct approach to chess: an independent analysis of the critical perception of comments, etc.

Classes were held twice a week. Among the participants were chess players Pisemskiy (KIM), Levitas (from state organizations), and others.

The I–II Category Matches

The Baku chess-checkers club organized a chess and checkers players match in Baku. The first-category players played against the second-category players.

The first day ended with the victory of the first-category checkers players in 5–2. The only match in the first category was won by Galicia L. Kupriyanov. The match between Zelikman and Rosenblatt ended in a draw.

The victory of Karlinsky over Levitas and Enver Shikhlinskaya, one of the strongest players in Azerbaijan in this championship, should be especially noted.

Guldin Lev Ýsayevich, born in 1916, was a master of sports in the USSR on chess since 1939, an engineer-telecommunicator, and a Baku Neftyanik champion in Azerbaijan, SSR.

JUDO

Samir Peysakhov was born on December 11, 1964, in Baku, Azerbaijan. He started playing football at the age of five. At the age of twelve, he decided to take up judo and has not stopped training since. After four years of intense judo training and at the age of sixteen, he became the champion of Baku in judo.

A year later, at the age of seventeen, he took first place in the Azerbaijan championship. He worked hard to improve his sportsmanship, and as a result, at the age of nineteen, he became the champion in the Transcaucasian district.

In 1996, his family came to the USA.

Samir Peysakhov has worked for many years as a judo coach. He brought up the winners of the American and Pan-American championships. Additionally, his students went on to become prize-winners of European international competitions, winners of Maccabi international competitions, and athletes who took part in the World Judo Championship.

At the moment, he trains more than one hundred students and continues to pass on his experience to a new generation of athletes because he finds this meaningful.

He lives in New York, USA, and he is an international-level coach with a sixth-degree black belt.

MORE ATTENTION TO CYCLING

Cycling has been cultivated in Baku for a long time, but noticeable changes in this area occurred only at the beginning of 1937. Unfortunately, the first trip of Baku cyclists to Union competitions gave poor results.

With the arrival in Baku of Svitsky (an athlete) in 1938, bicycle sports sharply stepped forward. Individual championships in Moscow in 1937 showed that cyclists from Baku were paid much attention. The All-Union Committee for Physical Education and Sports allocated eight seats, up from the previous year's three. T. Geits (from Dynamo) received a master's degree. However, the results of the competition showed that it would be difficult for the masters to retain the title in the near future.

FENCING IN BAKU

-

There are many fencers and even more people in Baku who want to get engaged in this sport. The fencing section at the Azerbaijan Committee of Physical Education and Sports has over ten instructors in fencing who know their job very well. M. Falkovskaya and M. Zinoveva will fight with swords.

FOOTBALL

-

Football Championship in the USSR, The Immortal Game

Minsk (Spartak)–Baku. The football team of Baku, Temp, met with Minsk Spartak at the stadium Dynamo in Baku on May 18.

Temp won 4–0.

This victory can be explained by the fact that the team was supplemented by such capable players as Alimkin, Rhine, etc.

FREE CALISTHENICS

Rhythmic gymnastics as a kind of sport appeared in the nineteenth century. The foundation and development of rhythmic gymnastics in Azerbaijan date back to the 1940s of the last century. Nadejda Merculova, who formed the first group of girls, played a great role in the formation of this sport. Under her leadership, gymnasts achieved great success in all-Union and international competitions. Larissa Zebina, Lina Vinnikov, Svetlana Senatorova, Nina Hajibeyli, Mila Shibaeva, and Elmira Hajiyeva were only some of those gymnasts.

SAILING

-

Ready to the Sea

The wind was storming the coastline of the Caspian Sea. The sea was covered with gray, foamy waves, advancing menacingly on the Grenade Barrier waterfront. Life on the ship was proceeding normally. The wind reached up to mark 7. The commanding staff of the Caspian Military Fleet decided to conduct a sailing competition. The terrible sea has its own laws. One sudden step may lead to inevitable failure and death. The rudders and sails were in the capable hands of strong competitors. Sailors Spivak and Bogorodsky passed the examination with "excellent marks."

SHOOTING

-

Competition of Shooters in Azerbaijan Championship

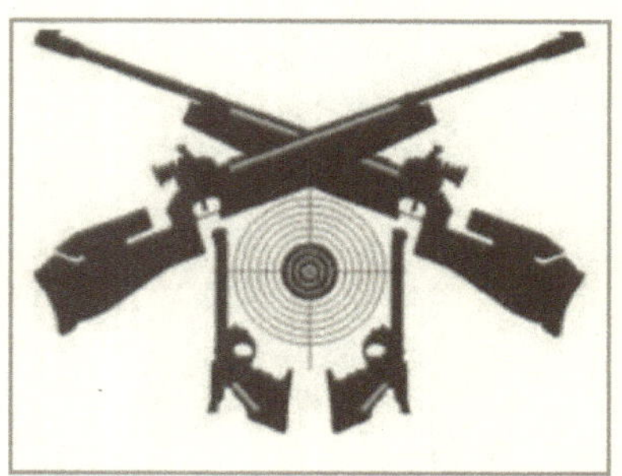

Shooting competitions and qualifying races were held in Baku for the Olympics in the USSR, which began in Moscow. The competition was attended by seventy-three people, including thirty-seven students from Baku and other regions of Azerbaijan.

To participate in the shooting sports day of the USSR in Moscow, Hyperboreysky, the most powerful member, entered the team of Baku and won first place.

SWIMMING

-

Success of Baku Swimmers

All Baku championships in swimming were held in the swimming pool of the cultural park Rothe-Fahne on the 22nd, 23rd, and 24th of September.

The competition was a great success. Swimmers made new achievements at every race. Twenty-two records for Azerbaijan were set. Particular success belonged to the young, well-trained swimmers Schultz and Zinoviev.

Two strong breaststroke swimmers—Schulze (AzGIFK) and the Carpenters ("sprits")—met at 200 meters. A fierce struggle between them began in the very first meter. At the first 100 meters, Schults went five feet ahead. In 150 meters, the gap increased to 5 pm. Here, Plotnikova changed to butterfly and breaststroke for a sharp finish. But Schulze, who could keep his strength, still managed to reach the finish line first. Her time of 3 minutes, 43.2 seconds became the new achievement in Azerbaijani sports.

The women's 200-meter backstroke passed interestingly. In the first swim, Schults beat the old record belonging to Azerbaijani sportsman Zinoviev, showing two minutes, 47, 9 seconds.

TUMBLING

-

Acrobatics is an ancient type of sport. The word "acrobat" comes from the Greek word *akrobates*, which means "rising up."

In the development of the sport in the nineteenth century, new acrobatic movements appeared, which were an integral part of the sport at that time.

The origins and development of acrobatics in Azerbaijan cover 1920–1930. G. Safarov, G. Bezhanov, Yurfeld Yu, D. Dvoryankin, I. Kiselev, and H. Agaev played a great role in the development of acrobatics in Azerbaijan in those years. In 1936, Baku hosted the first unofficial tournament, and only men's groups were included in this tournament. After that, Azerbaijani acrobats became involved in all-Union competitions.

VOLLEYBALL

Milman Lev Samuilovich was born in 1930 in the city of Baku, Azerbaijan. In 1951–1953, he played for the Azerbaijan national team. In 1953–1955, he played for the Sverdlovsk club Petrel. The team won a silver medal at the national championship in 1955.

In 1955–1961, he was the senior coach of the women's and men's volleyball teams at the Ural Polytechnic Institute. In 1961–1970, he was the senior coach of the men's volleyball team of the Azerbaijan State University of Oil and Industry.

The women's and men's teams of Azerbaijan also trained. Among his wards was Olympic and world champion Inna Ryskal.

In 1971–1972, he was invited to coach the AZS volleyball club in Olsztyn, Poland. Some players from the team were recruited for the Polish men's team, which became the 1976 Olympic champion.

**Coaching Boris Yeltsin, the former
President of Russia.**
Lev Miilman, third from right, poses in group
photo from 1950s, with the former President
of Russia Boris Yeltsin, third from left.

In 1972–1980, he was the head of the sports
department of the Azerbaijan State Oil Academy.
In 1980–1990, he was the deputy minister of
Sports Industry of the Republic of Azerbaijan. In
1990–2018, he was a volunteer assistant coach at
Springfield College.

WRESTLING

-

Burevestnik

The Central Council of Burevestnik (Thunderbird) in late November in Baku held a competition in French wrestling. Azerbaijan's Burevestnik for these events put forward its own team, which included

Bakhshaliyev, Goreloshvili, Movsumov, Lichtman, and others.

Section of Young Wrestlers

With the initiative of wrestling coach Anderson, the sports society "Builder" organized a teen section of French wrestling for the first time in Baku. There were eight sportsmen in the section, and Anderson had already spent two sessions.

TOC

-

The Jews in Sports

- Sports instructors

    1. À. Zamishvili
    2. G. Lubarskiy
    3. G. Vishnevskiy
    4. Â. Kogan
    5. À. Zinkoviskiy

- Sports photography

    1. À. Ginzburg
    2. V. Bedashvili
    3. V. Levit
    4. Ì. Levit

- Sports journalists

  1. À. Malinkovskiy
  2. R. Bazer
  3. Å. Lenskiy
  4. L. Esterkin
  5. V. Monastirskiy
  6. À. Golevskiy
  7. I. Galitskiy
  8. À. Olkhovskiy
  9. V. Sokolovskiy
  10. V. Grid
  11. Ì. Gilskiy
  12. N. Kobich
  13. I. Injashvili
  14. À. Bogod
  15. P. Bronin
  16. V. Romin
  17. G. Caspiyskiy
  18. Ì. Twanieshvili

- Sports judges

  1. À. Beylin
  2. Ì. Zorkin
  3. V. Lukshin

4.   V. Bragin

- Sports editors

  1.   B. Borukhovich

- Gymnastics

  1.   Ì. Rijanskaya
  2.   Ê. Iskinskiy
  3.   À. Sokhatskiy
  4.   N. Bats
  5.   Ê. Smoglovskaya
  6.   À. Saaliashvili
  7.   A. Shumanov
  8.   Y. Swiner
  9.   V. Tishner
  10. Jemanskiy

- Boxing

  1.   À. Goldshtayn
  2.   G. Steyn

- Heavy weight lifting

    1. À. Feorra
    2. À. Rapoport
    3. À. Shults
    4. V. Unikin
    5. I. Mercuris
    6. G. Dick
    7. G. Bromberg
    8. À. Tsamalashvili
    9. B. Beylin
    10. Å. Goxberg

- Athletics

    1. G. Urbanovich
    2. G. Ganeker
    3. Ò. Dmitrashvili
    4. À. Bergen
    5. V. Logvin

- Chess and checkers

    1. Rojdestvenskaya
    2. Polisskiy
    3. Lopatinskiy

4. Zelikman
5. Doktorskiy
6. Barinov
7. Rosenblatt
8. Sienkievich
9. Gegelgants
10. Krintsman
11. Pisemskiy
12. Levitas
13. Guldin
14. Zatulovskaya
15. Listengarten

- Cycling

    1. À. Geits

- Tennis

    1. V. Uskovskiy
    2. L. Esterkin
    3. V. Goldshtein

- Shooting

    1. Giperboreyskaya

• Swimming

1. Litvin
2. Atlas
3. Deykun

EPILOGUE

What else can I say? I am really proud of this project, and it was a pleasure to work with all those who helped me write this book. I have never tried to uplift one nation and leave the others in the shade of other people. I have always tried to express facts based on the concept of justice. In this book, the main thing is not the text itself, just as the sounding of musical notes in music is not the main thing.

REFERENCES

-

Becker, Moses. 2000. *Jews Azerbaijan: History and Modernity*. Baku.
State Archive of the Republic of Azerbaijan.
Sports newspaper published until 1939.
And old Baku Jews.

ABOUT THE AUTHOR

Asif Hidayat Oglu Bayramov is a writer, a master in sports sciences, a trainer, and a black belt holder in Judo. He was born in Armenia, a Muslim by faith, deported forcibly in 1988 to Azerbaijan, and suffered multiple discriminations. This deportation caused great emotional shock and motivated him to learn about the local cultures of different people who also endured discrimination and deportation. The major community among them were Jewish people, living at that time in Baku.

Asif dedicated his life to promoting friendship between Muslims and Jews. He organized an exhibition on Judaism in Baku and was a community organizer among Muslim and Jewish populations.

He worked for several years at the Israeli Consulate in Baku to prepare the children for immigration to Israel and military service there.

Asif Bayramov researched the lives of Jewish sportsmen in Azerbaijan. It was fascinating to explore the big contributions and achievements of Jewish athletes. He worked in archives, colleges, libraries, sports centers in Baku, and other cities, and interviewed many legendary Jewish athletes.

The results of his research, analysis of archives' materials, and interviews with many legendary Jews were summarized in several publications, including *Azerbaijani Jews in Sports*, first edition, which caused a good deal of interest in Azerbaijan, the United States, and Israel. The book received multiple positive reviews and letters of appreciation from the president and prime minister of Israel.

The first edition of *Azerbaijani Jews in Sports* was presented with great success in the Library of Congress (Washington, DC), the AJC, the Washington Mayor's office, and other organizations in America.

The current *Azerbaijani Jews* in Sports is the second edition and contains many new personalities, facts, and additional material.